Cornelius Hanko

Studies in 1 & 2 THESSALONIANS

REFORMED
FREE PUBLISHING
ASSOCIATION

Jenison, Michigan

Scripture cited is taken from the Authorized (King James) Version

Reformed Free Publishing Association
1894 Georgetown Center Drive
Jenison MI 49428
616-457-5970
www.rfpa.org
mail@rfpa.org

Book design and typesetting by Erika Kiel

ISBN 978-1-936054-52-7
LCCN 2014953051

Preface

Especially in the times in which we live, when so many signs point us to the end of the ages, the two epistles to the Thessalonians take on greater significance since they instruct us concerning the second coming of Christ.

Paul had sent Timothy to Thessalonica to ascertain the welfare of this newly organized congregation. Upon his return Timothy reported that they were growing spiritually so that their faith was known throughout the churches. But there were problems. Some in the congregation expected Christ to return in their day and even in the very near future. This had raised a question in their minds concerning those who die before the Lord's return and had also caused some to give up their work, sell their homes, and idle away the time while they waited for the day of Christ's coming.

These and other problems occasioned Paul's writing of the two epistles to the Thessalonians. The apostle would have gladly paid them a personal visit; but since this was impossible, he writes these epistles under divine inspiration, and they are preserved for our edification.

In the second epistle Paul thanks God for the spiritual advancement of the congregation. They were growing exceedingly in faith and were abounding in love toward one another and others of the household of faith. Even though they suffered severe persecutions and tribulations, they bore them patiently and stood firm in the truth (1:3–4).

But their original problem, mentioned in the first epistle, still persisted and was even aggravated. They were shaken in mind and troubled, possibly by a letter purported to have been sent from the hand of Paul (2:2). They had the mistaken idea that the day of the Lord had come (2:3). There were some among them who had become idle busybodies and dependent on others for their daily existence (3:11–13).

Especially important in the second epistle is the instruction concerning the future rise of false prophets, the apostasy that must come before Christ's return, and the man of sin who will appear in due time. The theme is the revelation of our Lord Jesus Christ at his coming.

As we prepare to study these epistles, we should bear in mind that we are treading on holy ground. We are dealing with the infallibly inspired scriptures, which must be considered reverently and accepted in simple child-like faith. When man speaks, we may disagree or contradict; when God speaks, we humbly listen. Moreover, God's word is the power unto salvation (Rom. 1:16), our spiritual meat and drink. We must search the scriptures with the prayer that we may live unto the praise of our God.

For your study it is important to have a Bible with references, a good concordance, a Bible dictionary, and a good commentary on 1 and 2 Thessalonians such as the *New Testament Commentary* by William Hendriksen.

Overview of 1 Thessalonians

Introduction

On his second missionary journey the apostle Paul, accompanied by Silas and Timothy, had labored for some time and had established a church in Philippi. Because of the persecution experienced there they continued on their journey to Thessalonica. Both Paul and Silas, having been beaten and imprisoned in Philippi, arrived in Thessalonica with fresh wounds they had received for the sake of the gospel.

Yet the apostle and his coworkers were ready to continue preaching the word also in Thessalonica until the persecution compelled him to leave. While Paul continued on to Berea, Silas and Timothy continued to labor for a time in the Thessalonian church and later joined Paul in Corinth. From Corinth Paul had sent Timothy to ascertain the conditions in the congregation of Thessalonica. As a result of Timothy's report Paul wrote 1 Thessalonians, the first of all his epistles.

Study Questions and Activities

1. Read carefully the entire epistle.

2. Study the map of Paul's second missionary journey. Locate Thessalonica.

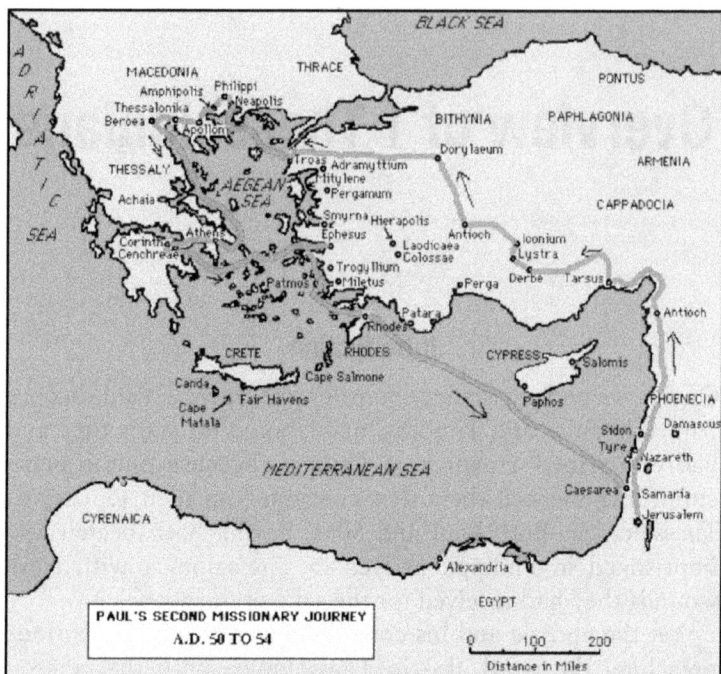

PAUL'S SECOND MISSIONARY JOURNEY
A.D. 50 TO 54

0   100   200
Distance in Miles

3. Where did Paul begin his labors in Thessalonica (Acts 17)?

4. Paul's preaching in Thessalonica

   a. What did Paul preach?

   b. Did some Jews believe and join Paul and Silas?

   c. Who also believed?

d. How long did Paul minister the word in Thessalonica?

5. Why was Paul forced to leave Thessalonica?

6. The congregation evidenced true faith and a sincere hope of eternal life (1 Thess. 1:3).

   a. To what does Paul ascribe this tremendous change from unbelief and idolatry to faith in the living God (1:4–6)?

   b. Was there evidence of a common bond with the other churches?

7. Labor among the Thessalonians (2:1–12)

   a. How had Paul and his coworkers labored among the Thessalonians?

   b. Of what had Paul and his coworkers been accused (2:3–6)?

   c. How was the Thessalonians' wholehearted reception of the gospel proof of Paul's sincerity as a true servant of Jesus Christ (2:12–14)?

d. What proof did the Thessalonians have that their faith was God's work of grace in them (2:14–20)?

8. Paul's concern for the congregation

   a. Why was Paul concerned about the congregation? What problems had arisen there (3:1–13)?

   b. What does Paul teach the members regarding a holy walk (4:1–2)?

   c. What does he say about brotherly love (4:9–12)?

   d. What problem had arisen concerning those who had died since coming to the faith (4:13–18)?

   e. Of what does Paul assure them?

9. What is our calling as believers who wait for the coming of the Lord?

10. What must be our attitude toward officebearers in the church (5:12–13)?

11. Sum up Paul's admonitions.

12. To what does Paul repeatedly refer, particularly at the end of almost every chapter?

"Peace I leave with you, my peace I give unto you: not as the world giveth, give I unto you. Let not your heart be troubled, neither let it be afraid."
—John 14:27

Greeting and Thanksgiving

1 Thessalonians 1

Introduction

In comparison with Paul's greetings in the other epistles, his greeting is very brief, showing that he is eager to get at the heart of his message to this newly organized congregation. The apostle mentions the senders, including Silas and Timothy, who must have known the contents of this letter. He also mentions the church that is brought into the fellowship of God and Christ. Then he pronounces the customary apostolic benediction: "Grace be unto you, and peace, from God our Father, and the Lord Jesus Christ."

He is thankful to God for the work of grace wrought in these believers. For here once more God had given evidence of his sovereign mercy and of the power of the gospel. The power of the gospel was evident in the preaching, for they were drawn from the worship of idols to serve the living God with the hope of eternal life. And this power was also evident in the believers themselves—in their works of faith, their labors of love, and their patient hope in the return of our Lord. Thus the word of the Lord sounded forth even to the saints throughout Macedonia and Achaia. (Look up these places on the map on page 6.)

At the same time the Thessalonian church became the object of persecution not only from the local Jews, but also from the unbelieving Gentiles, both of whom revealed themselves as enemies of the cross of Jesus Christ.

Study Questions and Activities

1. Read chapter 1.

2. Paul's greeting to the Thessalonians

   a. Compare this greeting with his greetings in other epistles.

   b. Is Paul's greeting a mere wish, or does it have apostolic authority in the name of Christ?

   c. Does the benediction in a divine worship service today have apostolic authority in the name of Christ? Why or why not?

   d. How are grace and peace related?

   e. When did Silvanus join Paul?

   f. What do we know about Silvanus?

   g. When did Timotheus join Paul?

   h. What do we know about Timotheus?

3. What is the church (Heidelberg Catechism, Q&A 54–55)?

4. A great wonder of grace had been wrought in the Thessalonian believers.

   a. What was this wonder of grace (v. 9; Heidelberg Catechism, Lord's Day 33; Canons of Dordt 3–4.11–12)?

   b. What threefold evidence of grace was manifest in the congregation (v. 3; 1 Cor. 13:13)?

   c. How was this grace wrought among them (v. 5)?

   d. What is the basis for their salvation (v. 4)?

5. The external and internal call of the gospel

   a. What is the external call of the gospel?

   b. Is the external call the same as a general, well-meant offer of salvation? Explain.

   c. What is the internal call of the gospel?

   d. What is the fruit of the internal call (Rom. 10:8–17)?

e. What is true faith? What are its elements? (Heidelberg Catechism, Lord's Day 7)?

f. How can we be assured of our calling and election (2 Pet. 1:10)?

6. Paul and his coworkers were examples to the believers.

   a. How were they examples (v. 5)?

   b. How did the believers become imitators (v. 6)?

   c. What kind of joy filled the believers? (v. 6; 1 Pet. 1:8)?

   d. How did they become examples for others (vv. 6–9)?

7. What is Christian witnessing?

   a. Prove from scripture and the creeds our calling as believers to witness.

   b. Where should witnessing begin?

c. What should be the content of our witness?

d. Who are the objects of our witness?

e. In what manner should we witness?

f. Give some misunderstandings or errors that are prevalent today concerning witnessing.

9. At what cost had the Thessalonians received the gospel (v. 6)?

"But of him are ye in Christ Jesus, who of God is made unto us wisdom, and righteousness, and sanctification, and redemption: That, according as it is written, He that glorieth, let him glory in the Lord."
—1 Corinthians 1:30–31

Paul's Defense
of His Preaching

1 Thessalonians 2:1–12

Introduction

Verse 1 of this chapter can more accurately be translated as "For ye ourselves, brethren, know our entrance in unto you, that it was not empty handed." The emphasis is on the treasure that Paul and his fellow workers carried with them: the free gift of God unto salvation (2 Cor. 4:7). They had a message that, in spite of all opposition, they were impelled by the zeal of God to proclaim.

Both the unbelieving Jews and the pagans sought to undermine Paul's preaching by bringing false accusations against him and his coworkers. They brought three charges against them: their message was no different from the vain philosophies of others; they exploited the church for personal gain; and their walk of life was not beyond reproof.

In these verses the apostle answers these charges, not because he wishes to defend himself, but because he wants no discredit to be brought upon the gospel.

Study Questions and Activities

1. Read chapter 2.

2. Opposition to the labors of Paul and his coworkers

   a. Who were the main opponents of Paul on the mission field, even as in Thessalonica (Acts 17:5)?

b. Is the false church always the greatest enemy to the people of God?

c. Will the false church be the greatest enemy of the people of God at the end of time? Prove your answer from scripture.

d. How does Paul sum up opposition in 2 Corinthians 4:8–12?

e. Which of the three charges mentioned in the introduction are found in verses 3–6?

f. Which charge is mentioned in verse 9?

3. Paul's defense of his ministry among the Thessalonians

a. How did Paul's experience in Philippi prove that he was not seeking personal gain (v. 2)?

1) How else did Paul show that he and others were not exploiting the church (vv. 3, 5)?

2) What was Paul's occupation (Acts 18:3; 2 Thess. 3:8)?

3) Would it have been wrong for Paul to expect the church to support him (Luke 10:7)?

4) In what sense was the apostle out to "get" the Thessalonians (v. 8)?

b. How does the apostle show that he was aware of the seriousness of his calling to preach the gospel (v. 3; 1 Tim. 1:11–12)?

1) How is the preaching of the gospel distinctive (Rom. 1:16; 10:15; 1 Cor. 1:18)?

2) *Preached* in verse 9 refers to proclaiming or heralding the gospel, even as a king's herald proclaims the message of the king in the exact words, tone of voice, and inflection of the king. What words does Paul use in 1 Thessalonians 1:5 and 2:2–4 to refer to his preaching?

3) How else does Paul describe his ministry (v. 7)?

4) How does he defend his ministry in verses 10–12?

5) Distinguish carefully between the three words, *exhorted, comforted, and charged*, used in verse 11.

c. Why are those who defend the truth of the gospel hated?

"But God forbid that I should glory, save in the cross of our Lord Jesus Christ, by whom the world is crucified unto me, and I unto the world." —Galatians 6:14

Lesson 4

The Thessalonians' Reception of the Gospel

1 Thessalonians 2:13–20

Introduction

The apostle continues his defense of the gospel over against the Gentiles and the unbelieving Jews in Thessalonica who were opposing the word of God by raising false accusations against Paul and his fellow workers.

Even as the gospel had been a power unto salvation elsewhere, so also in Thessalonica. The believers' embrace of the gospel was proof of its power.

Paul writes verses 17–20 under great stress. It appears that he had been accused of lack of concern for the congregation, since, instead of returning to them, he had sent Timothy to visit them. To this charge the apostle answers that he was torn from them like an orphan from its parents and that he would gladly have returned to them, even as he carries the church in his heart, but Satan hindered him.

The last part of verses 19–20 can be paraphrased as "For who is our hope, or joy, or glory-wreath? others only? Indeed, you also who are our glory in the presence of the Lord at his coming."

Study Questions and Activities

1. Read chapter 2.

2. The effectual power of the word

    a. What does Paul say in verse 13 regarding the distinction between the word preached and the effectual working of that word?

b. What is the difference between the external call and the internal call by the word?

c. In verse 13 how could Paul speak of his preaching as "the word of God" (Gal. 1:1)?

d. Is this true of the preaching of ministers today (Rom. 10:13–15)?

e. What makes the preaching of the word a power of God unto salvation to every one who believes (Acts 16:14; Rom. 1:16)?

f. What is the opposite effect on those who reject the word (John 9:39; 1 Pet. 2:7–8)?

g. How were the believers in Thessalonica followers (imitators) of the churches in Judea (v. 14)?

3. Willingness to endure persecution is a mark of true discipleship.

a. Prove the above statement.

b. Why should believers be willing to accept persecution (Phil. 1:29)?

c. Find other scriptural references to prove that believers should willingly accept persecution.

d. Was persecution in the homes of the Thessalonians (Acts 17:4)?

e. What was the calling of the believing wife (1 Pet. 3:1–4)?

f. What was the past history of those who instituted persecution in Thessalonica (v. 15)?

g. Why did they now persecute the believers in Thessalonica (v. 16)?

h. How were the persecutors "contrary to all men" (vv. 15–16)?

i. In what sense is the wrath of God on the Jews now and eternally (Rom. 9–11)?

j. Is there a remnant of the Jews saved in the new dispensation?

4. Paul's absence was not due to an "out of sight, out of mind [heart]."

   a. How does Paul show this to the believers in Thessalonica?

   b. Although Satan tries to hinder the gospel, is he able to prevent it from serving its purpose?

   c. Is Satan included under the providence of God (Heidelberg Catechism, Lord's Day 10)?

   d. Give at least three reasons Paul and his fellow workers desired to return to the church of Thessalonica.

   e. Did Paul ever return to that church (Acts 20:1)?

   f. What does it mean that the Thessalonian church, along with other churches, was Paul's "joy"?

   g. What does Paul mean when he refers to these churches as his "hope" and "crown"?

5. Do we expect a victor's crown? Prove from the scriptures.

6. Who receives the glory in the world to come (Rev. 4:10)?

"For this cause also thank we God without ceasing, because, when ye received the word of God which ye heard of us, ye received it not as the word of men, but as it is in truth, the word of God, which effectually worketh also in you that believe."—1 Thessalonians 2:13

Paul's Response to Timothy's Report

1 Thessalonians 3

Introduction

The apostle says, "we could no longer forbear." After a short term of labor, he had been compelled to leave the congregation and to entrust them to the care of Silas and Timothy. Later they also left to join Paul. Meanwhile the newly organized church suffered severe persecution from the enemies of Christ and the gospel. Even deceitful flatteries were used to lure the believers from the faith. This caused Paul great concern for their spiritual welfare. Were they spiritually strong enough to withstand all this opposition?

Therefore, in his great love for the congregation, even at the expense of being left alone for a time, he had sent Timothy to inquire as to their welfare. Was Silas with Paul? Or had he been sent elsewhere? To Philippi possibly? We do not know. Now Timothy had gone to Thessalonica and had returned with a favorable report. There were problems, deficiencies, but spiritually the congregation had prospered even under severe trials.

This quickens Paul with new zeal and thankfulness. He feels himself inadequate to give full thanks to God for the wonders of his grace. Paul prays that he and his fellow workers may return to the congregation, but if not, he still asks that they may increase in love even unto the return of Christ with all his saints.

Study Questions and Activities

1. Read the entire epistle.

2. The apostle's love for the congregation

   a. Why did Paul send Timothy to the church at Thessalonica?

      1) What recommendation did Paul give to this young coworker who comes to them alone (v. 2)?

      2) What does Paul commission Timothy to do (v. 2)?

      3) Paul adds in verse 5: "I sent to know your faith, lest by some means the tempter has tempted [lured] you, and our labour be in vain." Is there a falling away of saints? Or did Paul seek assurance that their faith was genuine and withstood the test (Canons of Dordt 5.8)?

   b. Why should not they and we be moved, that is, disturbed or troubled when we are persecuted for our faith (v. 4)?

      1) What does Acts 14:22 teach regarding persecution?

      2) What does it mean that we are "appointed" unto afflictions (1 Cor. 4:9)?

3) In what special sense was this true of the apostles (1 Cor. 4:9)?

4) Had Jesus, as well as Paul, warned them and us of this? Prove your answer.

c. Upon his return, what favorable report had Timothy given (v. 7)?

d. Timothy had also reported a lack in the Thessalonians' faith. What was lacking?

   1) What does Paul mean when he says, "For now we live, if [since or when] ye stand fast in the Lord" (v. 8)? Does chapter 2:19–20 shed light on this?

   2) Why does Paul in verse 9 put his thanks in the form of a question: "What thanks can we render?"

   3) Is his joy merely natural? Or spiritual? Prove your answer.

3. Paul's prayer that God may direct his way that he may once more labor among them becomes a benediction.

a. What is Paul's desire for the church?

b. To whom does "all men" refer? Note that *men* is in italics (v. 12).

c. What ultimate goal did the apostle seek for the church?

d. What does it mean that Christ will be coming "with all his saints" (v. 13; Rev. 19:14 in connection with 7:9)?

e. Do not fail to notice Paul's repeated reference to the *parousia* at the end of some chapters. What is the significance of this?

"And the Lord make you to increase and abound in love one toward another, and toward all men, even as we do toward you."—1 Thessalonians 3:12

An Exhortation to Sanctification

Thessalonians 4:1–12

Introduction

Thessalonians 4 begins a new section of the epistle that consists of admonitions and instructions, the latter particularly in regard to the return of our Lord.

The apostle bases his admonitions on his apostolic authority, which Christ had laid upon him, and appeals to the Thessalonians' efficacious calling out of darkness into God's light. They are made saints in Christ Jesus and are therefore responsible to God for their walk of life.

Paul admonishes them to live as renewed saints within the marriage bond, putting off the old man of sin along with the immorality they once practiced. He also warns them not to defraud the brother. This can be taken in the broader sense, as a warning against defrauding the brother in business. In the context it more likely refers to defrauding the brother by taking his wife.

Paul warns that immorality is not only a sin against our fellow believer but also is sin against the most high God, who is the avenger of all evil in this life and in eternity.

In verses 9–12 Paul urges the saints, in order to grow in grace, to live in brotherly love one with the other. They must not be fanatics, busybodies, or loafers, but by their godly walk they must give a good example to those within and outside the church.

Study Questions and Activities

1. Read chapter 4.

2. Walking in sanctification

   a. What is sanctification? Look up the definition in Herman Hoeksema, *Reformed Dogmatics*.

   b. Since sanctification means "to be holy, even as God is holy," what two elements are implied in holiness?

   c. According to Ephesians 4:22–24 what does sanctification include?

   d. If sanctification is the work of God's Spirit in our hearts, why are we called *to walk in* sanctification (Rom. 6:12–16; Canons of Dordt 5.4)?

3. Abstaining from fornication and living sanctified in marriage

   a. What is the distinction between fornication and adultery?

   b. Why are particularly fornication and adultery mentioned to those who recently came out of heathendom?

   c. Why is it so very important to seek a God-fearing mate?

   d. What does scripture say about seeking a God-fearing mate?

e. What is the meaning of the phrase "to possess his vessel in sanctification" (v. 4)?

f. How does possessing one's vessel in sanctification apply to all marital relationships?

g. How does Paul distinguish a godly relationship from the marital relationships of those who do not know God?

h. How is there danger that we could be guilty of "the lust of concupiscence" (v. 5)?

i. What is the relationship between the lust of concupiscence and the many divorces of our day?

j. Are these sins signs of the times? Find scriptures to support your answer.

k. How must the husband honor his wife in the marriage relationship?

l. Is the wife God's gift especially for her husband?

m. How can a husband dishonor his wife?

n. The King James translation leaves the impression that the "defrauding" of the brother in verse 6 is in business, but according to the context it can well refer to marital relationships. In what ways can one defraud his brother?

o. What does Lord's Day 41 of the Heidelberg Catechism say about the evil of defrauding a brother?

4. Despising God's grace

   a. How do we despise God and his work of grace when we sin (v. 8)?

   b. Do God's admonitions come to us as advice or as divine mandates? Prove your answer from scripture.

   c. Is God an avenger in this life? Give examples.

5. The walk of believers who have the love of God spread abroad in their hearts

   a. To what are believers admonished?

   b. What does it mean "to be quiet" (v. 11)?

c. What does it mean "to do your own business, and to work with your own hands" (v. 11)?

d. What does it mean to "walk honestly" (v. 12)?

e. Why is it necessary within the church "to be quiet,... to do your own business,...to work with your own hands," and to "walk honestly"?

f. Why is it necessary for those outside the church that believers live this way?

"Flee fornication. Every sin that a man doeth is without the body; but he that committeth fornication sinneth against his own body. What! know ye not that your body is the temple of the Holy Ghost which is in you, which ye have of God, and ye are not your own?"—1 Corinthians 6:18–19

The Final Resurrection

1 Thessalonians 4:13–18

Introduction

There was a misunderstanding among some in the congregation of Thessalonica regarding the second coming of Christ. Some expected that Christ should have returned or would return in the immediate future, even in their time. Their concern centered about their fellow believers who had already died. What would happen to them? Would they be at a disadvantage because they would not be living when Christ returned? Was there no hope for their sharing in the ultimate glory?

These questions the apostle answers in verses 13–18 of chapter 4. At the same time he casts light upon the events related to the second coming of Christ.

Study Questions and Activities

1. Read the entire chapter.

2. Those who are asleep

   a. To whom does Paul refer when he speaks of "them which are asleep" and "them...which sleep in Jesus" (vv. 13–14)?

   b. What is the theory of soul sleep?

c. Prove that the theory of soul sleep is wrong by showing from the scriptures that those who die in the Lord are now in a conscious state (Ps. 16:10; Luke 23:43; 2 Cor. 5:1; Rev. 20).

d. Look up Job 14:12; Acts 7:60; 1 Corinthians 11:30; 15:51–52; and 1 Thessalonians 4:13–18, which refer to "sleep."

   1) What does it mean that the departed believers "sleep"?

   2) Explain why the salvation of departed believers is not yet complete.

3. Show that the resurrection of believers necessarily follows from the resurrection of Christ (Heidelberg Catechism, Lord's Day 17). Find scriptural proof.

4. Christ's second coming

   a. Give the order of events at the second coming of Christ.

   b. What is meant by the sign of the Son of man (Matt. 24:30)?

c. How is the sign of the Son of man related to everything that follows it?

d. The Lord will descend "with a shout, with the voice of the archangel, and with the trump of God" (v. 16).

   1) What is meant by "with a shout"?

   2) How is the Lord's coming with a shout related to John 5:28?

   3) Who is the accompanying archangel (Dan. 10:13, 21; 12:1; Jude 9; Rev. 12:7)?

   4) What was the use of the trumpet in the old dispensation (Bible dictionary; Ex. 19:16–17, 19; 1 Cor. 15:52?

   5) What is the significance of the sound of the trumpet at Christ's second coming?

e. What does it mean that "the dead in Christ shall rise first" (v. 16)?

f. What will happen to those living at the moment of Christ's second appearance (v. 17; 1 Cor. 15:51–54)?

g. What is the meaning of "caught up together with them in the clouds, to meet the Lord in the air" (v. 17; Rev. 11:12)?

1) What is the premillennial theory of the "rapture"?

2) What is the significance of being "caught up together...in the clouds"?

3) What do the "clouds" symbolize (v. 17; Acts 1:9–11)?

4) How is verse 17 related to 1 Thessalonians 3:13 and 4:14?

5) What is the meaning of "so shall we ever be with the Lord" (v. 17)?

6) Why is being with the Lord so important to us?

5. What is the purpose of Christ's return (Matt. 25:31–46; 2 Thess. 1:7–9; Rev. 19:7–9; 21:2)?

6. Of what great danger did Jesus warn his disciples concerning his second coming (Matt. 24:42, 44; 25: 1–13)?

a. What should be our attitudes toward the second coming of Christ?

b. How do our attitudes toward the second coming of Christ control our lives in the world?

c. What comfort do you derive from Christ's return (Heidelberg Catechism, Q&A 52)?

"Therefore, my beloved brethren, be ye stedfast, unmoveable, always abounding in the work of the Lord, forasmuch as ye know that your labour is not in vain in the Lord."—1 Corinthians 15:58

Christ's Sudden and Unexpected Return

1 Thessalonians 5:1–11

Introduction

The subject treated in the last part of chapter 4 is continued in 1 Thessalonians 5:1–11. The apostle recognizes impatience in the believers occasioned by the severe persecution to which they were subjected and the mistaken notion that Christ should have returned already.

They must have asked, "When will Christ return, and how will that coming be?" Paul answers that these questions are of less importance, but watchfulness is far more important. We must always be on our guard, ready and eager for our final salvation.

Study Questions and Activities

1. Read chapters 4 and 5.

2. The time and manner of Christ's return

   a. Can we know the exact time Christ will return (Acts 1:7; Matt. 24:36, 43–44)?

   b. What does it mean that "Christ so cometh as a thief in the night" (Matt. 24:43; 2 Pet. 3:10; Rev. 3:3; 16:15)?

c. For whom will Christ's coming be sudden and destructive (v. 3; Matt. 24:37–44; Luke 17:26–30; 2 Pet. 3:1–10)?

d. What does the figure of a woman in travail signify in this connection (Ps. 48:4–8; Rev. 6:12–17)?

e. Does the figure also have a more favorable meaning (John 16:21–22)?

3. Contrast between believer and unbeliever

a. What contrast does Paul draw between the believer and the unbeliever (v. 4)?

b. What is meant by the "night" in contrast to the "day" (vv. 4–5)?

c. What is the "darkness" in contrast to the "light" (John 11:10; Eph. 5:8; 1 John 2:11)?

d. What admonition comes to the children of light (vv. 6–7; Matt. 25:1–13; Luke 21:34, 36; 1 Pet. 5:8)?

4. What is included in sobriety? (v. 8; 1 Cor. 13:13; Eph. 6:10–18)?

5. What three incentives does Paul give for believers to watch in sobriety (vv. 2, 9–10)?

6. What double admonition follows in verse 11?

"Watch ye, stand fast in the faith, quit you like men, be strong. Let all your things be done with charity."—1 Corinthians 16:13–14

Final Admonitions and Benediction

1 Thessalonians 5:12–28

Introduction

These final admonitions are a continuation of those given in chapter 4:1–12. Yet they are also closely related to and follow out of the admonitions in the first part of chapter 5 to be sober and to watch for the coming of the Lord.

Living in eager expectation for the Lord's return carries with it the duty to be ready at all times to give a reason of the hope that is within us (1 Pet. 3:15). Therefore these admonitions follow the others.

Study Questions and Activities

1. Read chapter 5.

2. What must be our attitude toward the elders in the church (vv. 12–13; 1 Tim. 5:17; Heb. 12:14; Heb. 13:17)?

3. "Peace among yourselves"

   a. What is meant by being "at peace among yourselves" (vv. 13–14)?

   b. What does 2 Thessalonians 3:11–12 say about the unruly (disorderly)?

c. What does Isaiah 35:3–4 and 43:1–7 say regarding the feebleminded (fainthearted)?

d. How does peace among yourselves apply to the weak (Rom. 14:1–19; 15:1–7; Col. 3:12–13)?

4. Verses 16–18 belong together. How are they interrelated with Luke 18:1–8, Romans 8:31–39, 1 Peter 1:6–8, and 1 Peter 2:9?

5. Verses 19–22 are also closely related.

   a. Is quenching the Spirit (v. 19) the same as grieving the Spirit (Eph. 4:30), or does it refer to the special gifts of the Spirit in the early church (1 Cor. 12, 14)?

   b. Why do we no longer have these special gifts?

   c. How is despising prophesying one manner of quenching the Spirit (1 Cor. 14:1–5)?

   d. What does it mean to prove all things and hold fast that which is good (Matt. 24:24; 1 John 4:1)?

e. Abstain from all appearance of evil. This has been taken to mean be on your guard when temptation lifts its vile head. Yet the meaning is avoid every form of evil (1 Cor. 10:31–32). Prove this meaning from other passages of scripture.

6. The conclusion begins with a benediction, a prayer that the God of peace will sanctify his church unto the final perfection in glory.

   a. What peace does the God of peace give us (Phil. 4:7)?

   b. How is that related to our sanctification?

   c. Paul desires that sanctification (making holy) be very thorough ("through and through"), including body, soul, and spirit (the whole person). It is God's work that carries on throughout our lives. How is sanctification related to 1 Thessalonians 4:13–18 (2 Pet. 1:10)?

7. Concluding remarks

   a. How is verse 24 a comfort to the believer?

   b. What is the comparison of verse 25 with 2 Thessalonians 3:1?

c. What did the holy kiss signify?

d. Do we have something similar to the holy kiss today?

e. Why is the apostle insistent that all shall know what he has written (v. 27)?

"Now unto him who is able to keep you from falling, and to present you faultless before the presence of his glory with exceeding joy, To the only wise God our Saviour, be glory and majesty, dominion and power, both now and ever. Amen."—Jude 24–25

Overview of 2 Thessalonians

Introduction

The theme of the second epistle to the Thessalonians is the revelation of Jesus Christ at his second coming. Moreover, since we live near the end of the ages, our times require us to recognize the present signs of Christ's coming and to learn to wait and to watch, so that when he comes he finds us ready and waiting.

Study Questions and Activities

1. Read 2 Thessalonians.

2. The greeting

   a. Compare Paul's greeting with that in 1 Thessalonians 1:1.

   b. Compare the greeting in 2 Thessalonians with 1 Peter 1:1–2.

3. Paul's expression of thanks

   a. In what three aspects had the congregation grown spiritually (1:3–4)?

b. What had been their reaction to persecution and tribulation (1:4)?

4. God's righteous judgment (1:5–12)

   a. What is God's righteous judgment upon his faithful church (1:5, 7, 10)?

   b. What is God's vengeance upon those who persecute the church (1:6, 8–9)?

   c. What two things does Paul desire in his prayer for the congregation (1:11)?

   d. What is his chief desire in this prayer (1:12)?

5. Events preceding Christ's second coming (2:1–12)

   a. What was the occasion for Paul's writing concerning the events of Christ's second coming (2:2)?

   b. What was the concern in the congregation (2:2)?

   c. What must happen before the Lord returns (2:3)?

d. How will the man of sin be recognized (2:3–4)?

e. Why has the man of sin not yet appeared (2:7)?

f. How will the man of sin expose the unbelievers (2:9–12)?

g. What is his end (2:8)?

6. For what does the apostle give thanks (2:13–14)?

7. To what does he admonish the believers (2:15)?

8. What is his request for them (2:16–17)?

9. Final admonitions
   a. What does Paul desire of the Thessalonians (3:1–2)?

   b. What does he command them (3:6–10)?

   c. What must be done to those who walk disorderly (3:11–15)?

10. What is the apostle's final benediction (3:16–18)?

"But we are bound to give thanks alway to God for you, brethren beloved of the Lord, because God hath from the beginning chosen you to salvation through sanctification of the Spirit and belief of the truth."
—2 Thessalonians 2:13

Lesson 11

Paul's Greeting and Encouragement

2 Thessalonians 1

Introduction

After his customary greeting Paul expresses his thanks to God for the splendid spiritual growth of the brethren in the church of Thessalonica. They were suffering persecution and tribulations, yet they had served to strengthen their patience and faith.

The congregation is assured of the righteous judgment of God upon them and upon those who persecute them. For the members of the congregation, God's judgment is a sure sign that they are considered worthy to be called children of the kingdom. And when Christ appears in heavenly majesty, he will be glorified in and with all the saints. Regarding the persecutors, God will "oppress the oppressors" with everlasting banishment from his presence and glory, because they obeyed not the gospel. The church is comforted in that Christ is glorified also in them.

Study Questions and Activities

1. Read chapter 1.

2. Salutation and thanksgiving

   a. What does it mean that the church is in God the Father and in the Lord Jesus Christ (Eph. 1:3–4, 7, 11; Heidelberg Catechism, Q&A 1)?

1) What is included in God's gift of grace to his church (Eph. 1:6; 2:7–8; 1 Pet. 4:10)?

2) What is meant by the peace mentioned in Paul's benediction (John 14:27; Rom. 5:1)?

b. The spiritual growth in the church (vv. 3–4)

1) How had the church grown spiritually?

2) Faith can be distinguished as the ability to believe and the act of believing. Is the ability a work of grace, and is the activity dependent on us (Canons of Dordt 3–4.12–14)?

3) What had Paul said about their charity in 1 Thessalonians 3:12; 4:9–10?

4) What is the difference between "endurance" and "preservation" (Canons of Dordt 5.8)?

5) How are "endurance" and "preservation" related (Canons of Dordt 5.8)?

6) What was the nature of the persecution in the Thessalonian church (1 Thess. 2:14–15)?

7) Show that the believers' suffering for Christ's sake is proof of their adoption and sonship (Matt. 5:10; Rom. 8:17; Phil. 1:29; 1 Thess. 2:14).

8) How does God reward the patience of the saints (Matt. 24:13; James 1:12)?

9) Is this a reward of their merit (Heidelberg Catechism, Q&A 63)?

3. What twofold manifestation of God's just judgment is mentioned in verses 5–10?

a. How does God justly reward our present suffering under persecution (v. 5; Rom. 8:17)?

1) What should be our attitude toward persecution (v. 7; Matt. 5:11–12; James 1:3–4)?

2) Of what do the persecutors of the church make themselves guilty (v. 8; Acts 9:4)?

3) In what sense do they "know not God" (v. 8; Acts 3:13–14; Rom. 1:18–20)?

b. To what does the revealing (lifting the veil) of the Lord refer (v. 7; 1 Thess. 4:16; Jude 14–15; Rev. 1:7)?

1) What tremendous contrast is drawn between unbelievers and believers in verses 9–10 (Rev. 5:11–13; 6:15–17)?

2) Who receives the glory in both believers and unbelievers (vv. 9–10)?

3) What will be the blessedness of the saints? (v. 10; Ps. 17:15).

4) To what should this arouse us (Rev. 22:20)?

c. What does it mean to be "count[ed] worthy of our calling" (v. 11)?

1) What is meant by the calling (1 Pet. 2:9)?

2) To what does God's goodness refer (Herman Hoeksema, *Reformed Dogmatics*)?

3) What is meant by God's "goodness" in verse 11?

4) What must be the goal of our lives (v. 12)?

"Wherefore also we pray always for you, that our God would count you worthy of this calling, and fulfill all the good pleasure of his goodness, and the work of faith with power: That the name of our Lord Jesus Christ may be glorified in you, and ye in him, according to the grace of our God and the Lord Jesus Christ."—2 Thessalonians 1:11–12

Events before Christ's Return

2 Thessalonians 2:1–6

Introduction

The church at Thessalonica had been shaken and troubled by those within the congregation who had drawn a wrong conclusion from the instruction of Paul in his first epistle concerning the return of Christ, particularly in 1 Thessalonians 2:19 and 5:1–11, and the meeting together at the moment of Christ's arrival of those who sleep and of those who are still alive (1 Thess. 4:13–20). Some had allowed themselves to be deceived as if the day of the Lord had already arrived, with serious consequences in the life of the congregation.

It is possible that there even was a letter purporting to be from the hand of the apostle that encouraged this idea. Some in the church may have thought that the Holy Spirit had given them some special revelation concerning Christ's coming (2 Thess. 2:2). In any case, Paul asks, "Remember ye not, that, when I was with you, I told you these things?" (v. 5).

Two important events must take place before the end, namely, the great apostasy and the reign of the antichrist. He now enters into more detail to instruct them concerning these matters.

Study Questions and Activities

1. Read 2 Thessalonians 2:1–6.

2. What does Paul call apostasy in verse 3?

   a. What did Jesus foretell in Matthew 24:11?

      1) Since a prophet is called of God and speaks the word that God lays in his mouth, what characterizes a false prophet?

      2) There were false prophets in the Old Testament (Jer. 14:14). Find other examples in scripture of false prophets.

      3) Were there false prophets in Paul's time (Acts 13:6)?

      4) Do the false teachers arise out of the world or out of the church?

      5) What false teachings are prevalent today?

   b. Of what does Christ speak in Matthew 24:24?

      1) How is Christ described in Philippians 2:9–11?

2) Should the pope be classified as a false christ? Why or why not?

3) Give some evidences of false christs in our day.

4) What is Christ's warning concerning these deceivers?

c. Of what does Jesus warn in Matthew 7:15?

1) When we speak of "liberals" in the church, do we mean that they are false teachers?

2) Is it right to compromise the truth in order to attain outward unity and peace?

3) What is the basis of unity and peace?

3. The man of sin represents the culmination of the sin of mankind since paradise (v. 3). He is the "mystery of iniquity [lawlessness]" (v. 7), that Wicked (v. 8).

a. He is also called "the son of perdition," born out of perdition and working only perdition (loss or destruction). For reference see Herman Hoeksema, *Behold He Cometh!* and Barry Gritters, *Antichrist.*

1) How is the man of sin pictured in Daniel 7:8?

2) What is he called in Matthew 24:15?

3) What is he called in 1 John 2:18, 22?

4) What does the term in 1 John 2:18, 22 mean?

5) Should we be on our guard against antichristian powers working in the church today?

6) How is the man of sin described in Revelation 13:2?

7) Will the antichrist be a political as well as a religious power (Dan. 7:25; Rev. 17:7–15)?

8) Is it possible that the pope might be the antichrist? Why or why not?

b. How does Paul describe the man of sin in 2 Thessalonians 2:4?

c. How does Daniel describe him in 7:25?

d. How is the man of sin described in Revelation 13:2?

"Wherein ye greatly rejoice, though now for a season, if need be, ye are in heaviness through manifold temptations."—1 Peter 1:6

Antichrist's Restraint and Deception

2 Thessalonians 2:7–12

Introduction

Paul begins these verses with a mention of the restraint of the antichrist. It must be admitted that, although the Thessalonians knew, we do not know who restrains him until the proper time for his appearance.

Some have thought that this restraint refers to God or to the Holy Spirit, or more particularly, to the restraint of sin in the hearts of wicked men (the second point of common grace). We can agree with Calvin that "God would not have spoken of the Spirit in enigmatic terms."

Study Questions and Activities

1. Read chapter 2.

2. The restraint of antichrist

   a. What outward restraint did God send at the time of the tower of Babel? (Gen. 11:1–10).

   b. What has prevented the appearance of the antichrist (Heidelberg Catechism, Q&A 27–28)?

c. What is the meaning of "he who now letteth will let, until he be taken out of the way" (2:7)?

d. What is one definite reason the antichrist has been prevented from appearing (Matt. 24:14)?

3. The deception of antichrist

   a. Who gives antichrist his authority and power to deceive (v. 9; John 8:44; Rev. 13:4)?

   b. How does antichrist deceive the people (Ex. 7:22; 8:7, 18; Matt. 24:24; Rev. 13:12–15)?

   c. Are his wonders real or only cunning tricks?

   d. What is the purpose of antichrist's deception?

   e. What other scriptural examples are there of magicians' performing wonders?

   f. Show how God is sovereign over deception (vv. 10–12; 1 Kings 22:19–23; Job 1:6–12; 2:1–6).

4. Destruction of "that Wicked"

   a. Who is meant by "that Wicked" (v. 8)?

   b. How will "that Wicked" be consumed and destroyed?

   c. What does this mean?

   d. What other scriptural passages speak about this?

5. Susceptibility for deception

   a. Why are some made susceptible for deception (vv. 10, 12)?

   b. How are walking in error and living in sin related (Matt. 24:11–12)?

   c. Mention evidences of delusion in our time.

6. Trial of the believers

   a. How will the believers be sorely tried (Matt. 24:21–22; Rev. 13:15–17)?

b. How will they be able to recognize the deceiver (Rev. 13:18)?

c. What does Jesus advise believers to do when they see the abomination of desolation (Matt. 24:16–18)?

d. What does this mean for believers today?

e. Why are believers not deceived (Matt. 24:13, 24; 1 Pet. 1:5)?

f. What should be their attitude toward lawlessness— abortion, sex outside of marriage, homosexual practices, divorce, remarriage, and the like—evident in our day?

"And then shall that Wicked be revealed, whom the Lord shall consume with the spirit of his mouth, and shall destroy with the brightness of his coming: Even him, whose coming is after the working of Satan with all power and signs and lying wonders."—2 Thessalonians 2:8–9

Lesson 14

Chosen to Salvation

2 Thessalonians 2:11–17

Introduction

We must not fail to notice the contrast between verses 11 and 13. Paul distinguishes, first, between the elect and the reprobate, those beloved of God from eternity and those who are hated in their sin. Second, he distinguishes between those who embrace the truth and those who reject it because they do not love it. Third, he distinguishes between those who are sanctified by the word and those who are hardened in their sin. The fourth distinction is between those who are saved and those who are damned.

To put at ease and to encourage those in the congregation who had been upset and troubled by the thought that the day of the Lord had already come, the apostle concludes chapter 2 with an admonition to remain steadfast in the faith.

Study Questions and Activities

1. Read chapter 2.

2. What are the two parts of God's eternal predestination?

   a. Who hold that God elects and reprobates on the basis of foreseen faith and unbelief (Canons of Dordt 1, error 3)?

b. Show that the doctrine of sovereign predestination is soundly scriptural (Rom. 8:29–30; 9:11, 13, 18; Eph. 1:5–6).

c. Should we consider eternal election and reprobation (predestination) to be a hard doctrine (Canons of Dordt 1.6)?

3. How does the preaching of the word separate between the elect and the reprobate (Matt. 13:24–30; 2 Cor. 2:15)?

a. What is the effect of the preaching upon those who believe (v. 13)?

b. What is the effect of the preaching upon those who do not believe (vv. 10–12)?

c. To what are we called (v. 14)?

d. What does this calling mean?

4. What word do the Canons of Dordt use for "stand[ing] fast" (v. 15; Canons of Dordt 5)?

a. Does "stand[ing] fast" or steadfastness mean that God holds us in his power, that we cling to God and depend on him, or that God holds us and gives us power to cling to him?

b. Does our perseverance depend in any sense at all upon us (Canons of Dordt 5.8)?

c. What is included in the admonition to "stand fast" (v. 15)?

d. What word is used for steadfastness in Psalm 62:8?

e. What word is used for steadfastness in Psalm 27:14?

f. What word is used for steadfastness in Mark 13:37?

g. What is the difference between the three different words for steadfastness?

5. What is meant by "everlasting consolation" (v. 16)?

a. What is our expectation after we die (Ps. 16:10; John 14:3; 2 Cor. 5:1)?

b. What is our hope for our bodies that rest in the grave (1 Cor. 15:42–44)?

c. What is the hope of those who are living when Christ returns (1 Cor. 15:51–54)?

d. What takes place when Christ returns (2 Cor. 5:10)?

e. Why is that a comfort for believers?

f. What will happen to this present creation (2 Pet. 3:10)?

6. What is included in our "eternal consolation" according to the Heidelberg Catechism Q&A 1?

a. How does this apply to our present suffering (2 Cor. 4:16–18)?

b. What does this mean for our future (v. 16)?

c. What incentive does this give us (v. 17; Heb. 4:11)?

"I had fainted, unless I had believed to see the goodness of the Lord in the land of the living. Wait on the Lord: be of good courage, and he shall strengthen thine heart: wait, I say, on the Lord."—Psalm 27:13–14

Lesson 15

Enduring Hope and Peace

2 Thessalonians 3

Introduction

We cannot fail to see in the last chapter of 2 Thessalonians the important relationship between God's work of grace in us and our resultant responsibility. The apostle certainly does not leave us with the impression that the operation of Christ's Spirit in our hearts deprives us of any human responsibility. The very opposite is true. Just as the Heidelberg Catechism concludes that our only comfort in life and death results in a life of thankfulness, so also Paul spurs us on as those who wait for the revelation of Jesus Christ to show in our lives the calm assurance, the steadfast endurance, and the abiding peace that we experience as God's gift to us. On the one hand the apostle writes, "The Lord is faithful, who shall stablish you, and keep you from evil" (v. 3). On the other hand he adds, "And we have confidence in the Lord touching you, that ye both do and will do the things which we command you" (v. 4).

In the first two verses Paul points out his need for intercessory prayer. In verses 3–15 he encourages the believers to walk in faith and be faithful to their calling over against those who lack the faith. And he concludes with the customary doxology (vv. 16–18).

Study Questions and Activities

1. Read chapter 3.

2. Paul asks for the intercessory prayers of the congregation.

   a. For what does the apostle desire intercession of the congregation?

   b. What does it mean for the word to have "free course," as it did in Thessalonica (v. 1)?

   c. How is verse 2 related to verse 1?

   d. Do Paul and his coworkers also make intercession for the Thessalonians (v. 5)? Find other examples in the two epistles.

3. The scriptures often admonish us to make intercessory prayers for others (1 Tim. 2:1–3).

   a. What are intercessory prayers?

   b. Find other places in scripture that admonish us to make intercessory prayers.

   c. Why must we make intercessory prayers?

4. Scripture also points out the benefits of intercessory prayers (James 5:16–17).

   a. Find other scriptural passages that give the benefits of intercessory prayers.

   b. What are the benefits of intercessory prayers?

5. Give examples from Paul's epistles that he made intercessory prayers for the churches.

6. How can the apostle be confident that the members of the church do and will endure opposition both from within and from without (vv. 3–4)?

   a. Sum up briefly what the Canons of Dordt say about the certainty of perseverance and enduring opposition (5:11–12).

   b. What is the difference between enduring and "patient waiting" (v. 5)?

   c. Why does the apostle admonish the believers to faithfulness when he is sure that God will work it in them (v. 5)?

1) How does Romans 1:16 apply to the above?

2) Find other scriptural passages that apply to the relationship between faithfulness and admonitions.

3) What does Canons 3–4.17 teach regarding the means of admonitions?

7. Dealing with those who walk disorderly in the church.

   a. Of what did those who walked disorderly in the church of Thessalonica make themselves guilty (vv. 10–11)?

   b. How should the Thessalonians deal with them (vv. 6, 14–15; 1 Cor. 5:11–12; 1 Thess. 5:14)?

   c. What is the meaning of "withdraw yourselves from every brother that walketh disorderly" (v. 6) and "note that man, and have no company with him" (v. 14)?

   d. Does Paul contradict the above instruction when he writes, "Yet count him not as an enemy, but admonish him as a brother" (v. 15)?

e. What is the relationship between "withdraw yourselves... note that man, and keep no company" and what Paul says in verse 15?

f. What did Jesus teach concerning those who walk disorderly (Matt. 18:15–17)?

g. Find other passages of scripture that instruct us regarding how to deal with those who walk disorderly in the church.

h. What is the teaching of the Heidelberg Catechism in Lord's Day 31, Q&A 84 concerning the relationship of the preaching of the gospel and Christian discipline?

i. What is the meaning in Lord's Day 31, Q&A 85 of "excluded from the Christian church, and by God himself from the kingdom of Christ"?

j. What is the purpose of Christian discipline (v. 14)?

k. Find other scriptural passages regarding the purpose of discipline.

l. What are the benefits of discipline for the one being disciplined?

m. What are the benefits of discipline for the church?

n. How had Paul and his coworkers been examples, even to those who walked disorderly (vv. 8–10; 1 Thess. 2:9–10)?

8. Paul's final benediction and signature

   a. What is a benediction?

   b. The peace of which Paul speaks is often confused with peace among individuals or nations (v. 16). Refute this idea.

   c. What is the peace of which the apostle speaks (Isa. 40:1–2; John 14:26–27; 16:33)?

   d. Why did Paul place his signature ("with mine own hand") at the end of the letter (v. 17)?

   e. Is there a connection between Paul's signature on this letter and what he says in 2:2: "by letter as from us"?

f. What is the importance of the benediction in Paul's letter to the Thessalonians?

g. What is the importance of benedictions in public worship?

"And we have confidence in the Lord touching you, that ye both do and will do the things which we command you. And the Lord direct your hearts into the love of God, and into the patient waiting for Christ."—2 Thessalonians 3:4–5

Notes

www.ingramcontent.com/pod-product-compliance
Lightning Source LLC
Chambersburg PA
CBHW060655030426
42337CB00017B/2623